1

This book is dedicated to

RED HAT LADIES

with sparkles in your eyes
crimson on your heads
smiles to brighten a day!
good friends in tow
nowhere special to go
Red Hat Ladies make a good show

Thank-you Red Hat Ladies!
The joy you share with your friends
rubs off on many around you!

Secrets Of The Craft Show Business

Written by: Robert M Secreti Jr.

Edited by: Alex Bodensieck

Photo Editor: Dillon Secreti

Copyright © November 23, 2009

Published by: The Beginning Shop

ISBN: 978-0-9777690-1-8

Printed in the United States of America

For more information contact:

bob@robertsecreti.com

www.robertsecreti.com

Robert Secreti

Po box 422

Burnt Hills N.Y. 12027

Chapter

Preface:

The intent of this book is to help new vendors, seasoned vendors and promoters alike to understand life inside the craft booth. Over the years there have been good intentioned caring people making good and bad decisions. This book has been written to help keep a great part of American history active and prosperous. The entrepreneur is alive and well.

Are you a person interested in looking for a way out from relying on Corporate America for their future?

The corporate giants have created a feeling within the work place that has employees, blue collar and white collar fighting for their quarterly survival. These in control people have a monster that is growing underneath them. Today, do you think it matters what you have done in the past for the betterment of the company? This new generation of companies has lost the understanding of what an employee and a company are all about. For the remainder of this book corporate economic control will be referred to as; "The Me Generation". Never mind the past. Who cares about next year? Let's do the quarter". They have forgotten what built this great nation, the loyal employee. These humans with fresh minds and loyal hearts only need steady work with a future. Today a job with a future is almost impossible to find and keep. The reason being is that it has come to be that the less people working, contributing, and growing with a business, somehow means more profits.

If you are in the automobile business how can you justify selling fewer cars to less dealers to make more money?

Isn't that what you are in the business to do, sell cars for money?

These thoughts may bring you to this point... If you are in control of even a small piece of a business be it cashier, sweeper, factory worker, manager, engineer all of us have a value.

By our hard work and efforts we create value for our company. This dollar value is a combination of your youth, health, brainpower, and let's not forget hard work. All of these things transform into profits. The profits are for your pocket, and for your boss's bottom line. The key elements here are brainpower and hard work. There are very few people that have tried to be an entrepreneur and just started collecting money.

It takes planning, thought, desire, commitment, and a dream. Just remember we would not have gotten to the moon if we didn't shoot for it. The idea here is to pick your goal and start shooting for it.

Look deep into your heart, or into the eyes of someone you care for. You have to want to make this change in your life.

Ask yourself, "Is there going to be something left for me when I get old? Will the government be able to take care of me when there are millions of nonworking elderly from the baby boomer generation retired, trying to get at their stocks?

Perhaps you don't want to think that far ahead or that deep. Good for you because let's not confuse the issue. We are only talking about starting a craft business. Yes, that's right, crafts, a year round business, or just for the summers. You can work weekends, holidays, middle of the week, whenever the buyers are there. Remember you need buyers. With this flexibility you can pick it. Do you want to work summers in the northeast, winters in Arizona? You decide. Remember always do a reconnaissance. Plan out your objective, define your plans. The more thought and planning you put into this the better you will be at making money.

Now remember it doesn't take a massive amount of money to do what we are going to talk about, only time and commitment.

After 28 years in the business there has not been a lot of money made. But it has allowed mobility and hours of enjoyment. The key thing here is enjoyment... You cannot turn this into drudgery.

"Buyers do not buy from losers..." Nor will they buy from a hungry pushy craft vender. You always want to portray a happy relaxed vendor that knows that the product being sold will always sell to the next buyer that comes through the tent. Remember you are going to be one of the last semblances of independent American owned and operated business, the future lies with you.

Wondering where the next craft show is going to be? Look in the paper; look on bulletin boards in your local supermarket. Don't be afraid to make a few phone calls. Just remember some of the folks putting on these shows really don't care if you sell anything or not … They are in the craft booth rental business. Just like PT Barnum said "There is a sucker born every minute." Sure they would like their vendors to make money but in most cases booth rentals are only there to raise money. Vendors come and go. Rarely will a vendor do lousy shows twice unless wasting time is part of the product. What I am trying to tell you is, be careful of all shows big ones, small ones, all shows. Now pay attention to this. If the Craft Business was lousy there would not be so many shows out there. Some small shows are excellent. What I mean by excellent, is the backbone of America, supported by hometown USA.

As we progress through these chapters we will be discussing my feelings and observations while engaging in the Craft Business. These ideas and thoughts could work very well for you too. Remember when you are with a buyer one misplaced word may blow a sale.

For the rest of this book the Craft Business will be referred to as a show.

The reason; it's your turn to shine and you are the star, "Lets Rock- n- Roll Baby".

Always Do A Recon

Considering a show, it is always best to surf an area. Today that just means, doing your homework. Take a drive, talk to acquaintances, get info, and get connected. Sometimes cruising through information really helps to sort things out.

While doing the recon get a feel for the community. What types of neighborhoods are there? Well-kept homes make a city or a neighborhood.

The exact show location is very important. Pictures will allow you to develop a strategy for the area. Remember understanding a show will always gain you more sales for the next show.

Once you get to the show site, cruise through the area. Look at the venders greeting them with a smile. See how friendly they are. Good venders are seasoned pros. Smiles are usually met with similar greetings. While scoping out the promoter; find out if they have a booth there. Look to see if they are selling a product or do they only sell show space. This tells you a lot about the promoter.

A craft-artisan type show seems to be better managed by someone that is on both sides of the show. They have a booth in the show so they know how well they are doing in the marketing.

They also understand the science behind running a good craft fair. A craft show is not a flea market. A craft show is not an antiques festival. Craft vendors/promoters tend to be more realistic in booth pricing. The bigger professionally promoted shows require you to hit the ground running. They make their money, you have to try and slice your share from the larger crowds.

Whenever possible, take time to talk to the venders. Ask questions, and be polite. Just remember a vender makes money by selling. Don't take up their valuable time with questions that could be answered with overall observation. Do not interrupt the vendor while there is a potential customer in the booth. Most venders are the friendliest souls on earth. When you are fact finding do some shopping. You as a vendor should support the commerce of this business.

During your travels always try to do as much shopping as you can. No one will ever complain about an American made gift.

There are a few standard questions that always should be asked while fact finding. Find out if the vendor did the show before. This fact can tell you how they did the prior year. A show with mostly new venders can mean that it is a lousy show. Veteran venders never return to an unsupported show. Did the community turn out? You can't always tell if a show was poor by the day's proceeds. Normally never judge a show until after the Christmas season. A lot of folks just enjoy browsing the shows thinking about the treasured gifts they are going to purchase at a later date. Always keep business cards handy. That does not necessarily mean right out in the open. Cards cost money. A show schedule is a good idea.

The schedule is more important to you than the customer. Here is why: it is your tool for organization. It will tell you ahead of time where you are going to be. How much inventory and what type you will need? It will keep you, your family, and friends updated so birthdays, weddings do not conflict. Planning ahead for the upcoming season is a smart idea. All the answers are not going to be in this book. For instance: Should I put the lighter tent up? How much should you talk to get the decision you are looking for? Maybe you are thinking about selling a good product at a sale price to interest buyers to consider other products? The most important part of being in business is decision making. Making the right decisions at the crossroads is what keeps us going forward. Remember, we are human and will make mistakes with perfect planning. Just not as many.

When you find a show with mostly new venders, try to find out why. The show could be new. Seasoned veterans tend to shy away from non-established shows unless they know the reputation of the promoter. Sometimes, for different reasons the shows location has been moved. Unfortunately, humans are creatures of habit. Move the show, change the date, it can upset venders and customers alike. New venders don't always mean a lousy show. That is up to you to try and figure out the show business. That is why you should always do a recon.

Most promoters do a very good job at setting up a show. If a show gets very little support from the locals is it going to be a bad show? All shows are designed to raise money for some type of event. Would you consider doing a show with new vendors? There have been shows that had two stages with different types of entertainment, good weather, well organized, yet no support from the community. Is it the promoters' fault? Many of the venders were new. The show was established through all the new venders that would sign up. The promoter raised the money for the civic organization through booth rentals. What do you do in a case like this? Enjoy all the entertainment and try to learn something.

Once you are at the perspective show take notice of the displays the venders presented to the public. Are they neat? The displays should be well organized. The treasures should be marked properly. Does the overall appearance show professionalism? Look to see how many displays look hokey.

One of the most important aspects of a successful show is if the venders at the entrance of the show represent good quality products. They can set the stage for the overall prosperity of the show. The travelers, shoppers, and browsers could pick up a frame of mind, from the first few vendors they see. They may retain this feeling for the remainder of the show. A good promoter will set the stage. Getting the word out to the people costs money. Some shows charge an entrance fee. Opinions vary about charging the public. Entry fees can regulate the type of attendance. Fees can help defray the show costs. They pay for advertising, and make money.

Another fact to look for is if the promoter has a following of venders.

Any show producer that can keep a good percentage of show people with them is a sure bet. There are many reasons to consider a possible show date. Here are a few: How much will the spaces cost you, the vendor? Not just in DOLLARS. Is there easy access for the vender as well as the treasure hunter? Some customers won't or can't climb stairs. They may not like to leave the happening area to shop. You want to be on the main floor, not off in the back, not downstairs. You want to be there on time ready and shining!

Check out set up times. Are they flexible? Remember, almost always you are traveling out of your element.

Set up times range. When a set up time is 8:oo am. You get there early at 7:30; they won't let you in to setup. It is nice to see flexible and early set up times. The set up is one of the most important parts to making or breaking the day's sales. Rigid set up/breakdown times can really restrict your ability to make sales. So be prepared when you're supposed to be. Try to shy away from rigid set up times. Remember, good and bad shows are eventful. Doing a methodical recon reduces unplanned events.

With booth cost, try to use the 10% rule. If a show costs $25 for a 10X10 space you should gross at least $250 in sales. If you pay $125 at a more expensive show, then only do $350 in gross sales, which can happen. What else could you have done? Well for starters, you could have done the $25 dollar show in a nice quaint community while staying at an Inn. Then had a nice dinner and probably spent less money. More times than not you could have done well over the 10% rule going to the less expensive show and had a great time doing it. Now don't misunderstand the thinking here, expensive shows have their place. This is why you should always do a recon. How much money do you want to gross? Remember when you do the large shows you are in the big time. Then plan, practice, and go for it. If there weren't big sales to make, there wouldn't be big shows.

To do well in the show business it requires a good philosophy on what making money is about. Always rate shows on comfort level versus dollars in sales. You can exchange amenities like ease of unloading / loading if the sales are there. How close are the comfort stations? Are they real clean? Does the show support basic vender life?

Look at the shoppers. Are they carrying shopping bags? Lots of bags means the patrons are supporting the show.

One thing that helps smooth out a show is a kid vender. Activity for the young ones can allow a few quiet seconds for Mommy and Daddy to think about the products before them.

Now let's talk about the types of venders we can encounter. Venders are a flavorful bunch. Face it, we are the show. What is the product? The product is what the show patron doesn't realize they came out to buy. Better said is, "What the show customer is intrigued to buy at the moment."

The vendors are the folks that give the treasure hunter what they want.

One excellent vendor that really made for a nice show was a day care center. They had a booth full of things for the kids to do for free, lots of simple ideas. There was a small swim pool. It had rocks in it with just enough water to wet a magnet on the end of a string attached to a stick. Little metal juice can tops with pictures painted on them lying in the pool. The little ones were lined up happy as clams to fish. There were also coloring stations, face painting and storytelling. There were plenty of simple inexpensive diversions for all.

My guess is the show promoter let this vender in for free due to the size of the setup. Who cares that they were promoting the day care center. This vender was truly an asset to this main street USA show.

While doing your recon, listen for conversations venders are having with their customers. Some venders are real pros AKA Showmen. Not only can they sell their products, folks just plain enjoy buying from them. Some people are naturals at selling. It really takes some seasoning to bring your prospective purchasers on a journey of enjoyment, spending their money. No one is telling you to entertain your patrons. A friendly smile with some enthusiasm behind it won't hurt.

There are all types of vendors; we will only be talking about a few. Now all of these showmen do well in sales. The question you need to answer is how well do you want to do? There are some vendors that have their booth set up so they can just sit there and collect money. Sure, you have seen them, sitting there cool looking. The booth is set up so that the shopper or browser can maneuver around the booth. The product sells itself. The only problem with this is; you can't work the crowd.

Always try to work the booth, moving to different spots adjusting the inventory. Humans are generally curious when there is activity going on. They can be drawn to the movement. Most times you can strike up a conversation with them if you are already standing.

Think about this for a moment. You are standing up working the booth, working the crowd. The strolling shopper comes in. You have a nice chat with them, maybe a sale maybe a tale. Next scenario: You are sitting down zoning out or reading a book. The strolling shopper comes in. You get up. The shopper gets nervous, clutches the purse. And then puts a hand in their pocket. Once that happens more than likely you will lose a chance for closing the sale. You never want the customer to tense up. Remember relaxing experiences harvest sales.

Now depending on what type of product you have to offer, check out the locations available to the venders. A lot of products don't do well next to food venders or entertainment. Try to sell fabrics, wood carvings, paintings or jewelry. It can be hard to sell products with smoke billowing into your space. Should your product require conversation to move it, loud music is out. There are a lot of products that will sell in this kind of environment, just manufacture more of an impulse product. Think about it the next time you go into public. Products used by us 21st century folks don't all have to be imported.

An important thing to remember is; while you are at each show, pick spots that you think will work well for you.

Then go find the promoter, and talk about your chances of getting one of your choices. Some show promoters will give you your choice if you pay a deposit or in full by a certain date. A lot of them will let you rent next year's space sometime during the show. If you do well at shows, always secure next year's space as soon as possible.

Well, you have traveled to the perspective show. You are loaded with information. Your head is full of pictures. You have taken notes. Ideas and thoughts are swimming through your mind. What are you going to do with this data? On your way home reflect on the day's events. Think about your conversations with the people you have encountered. What impressions are you bringing back with you? The best indicator is your gut feeling. In the end after all of this fact finding, if it feels good, you have laid out all the information and you like it, start planning.

There is a lot to think about when planning a show. There are questions you need to ask yourself. Is this show business going to be well planned and thought out or just a whim to try it out a couple of times? The amount of work you put into being a showman will show up on the other end in form of sales and enjoyment

Booth design and layout

Successful venders have a functional booth layout. Most show spaces are "10x10". You have to understand what 10x10 means. The square footage numerically comes out to 100sq feet. There are different categories, 10x10 inside, and 10x10 outside. Your booth design needs to be somewhat flexible. There are always obstacles inside or out. When you are inside there could be wall fixtures, structurally mounted furnishings, windowsills, doorknobs, you name it. You have to learn to adjust to these little appendages.

When you are outside, there are trees, mud, rocks, and natural grades. A flexible design could be in two-foot sections. Mostly all connections are made with bungees (flexible rubber things with hooks). You can't beat bungees, when they came out, "Why bungees changed my life."

No more drills, screws, or small attachments, just rubbery flexible bungees. Permanently screwed connections are fine, try to limit screwing and unscrewing at shows. Workable displays should just snap, snap together. Two-foot sections allow you the flexibility to work around obstacles unexpected when you get there. Bungees allow the display to sway and flex with the elements. Indoors or out there is always a chance that something or someone will be banging into your setup.

Booth sizes vary, there are usually single, double or triple offered. If you decide to go with a larger display area, remember you don't have to jam pack displays in the whole area. People tend to relax when they're not stacked like cordwood. Open and airy is always nice. Keep in mind that you also have to break down and load your materials after a long day.

Only have one person selling per 10x10 display, which gives more room for the shopper. Shoppers like to have their own space around them. In most cases they won't come in if they feel their personal space is violated.

Over time try variations within the booth area. A not too busy 3D layout can give you a nice look. Using this method gets more products within the 10X10 because you are also going up 4 feet. Always try to keep blind spots to a minimum. People see in depth. They like perspective. They hunt and gather by nature.

Some show folks prefer 3 tables with their displays on them. Again you need to put maximum effort into trying to find out what works the best for you and your sales. This is a business that changes from minute to minute. Every move or function should have a purpose. Normally you have around 5 hours per show to make it, and then it is off to your next jump. Two day shows are a lot more fun. You can settle into selling, without as much stress. If you live in an area where rain comes regularly, two day shows could get you one decent day. Rainy may not be a bad thing. There are a lot of people that enjoy a walk in the rain. It may surprise you how many folks show up to shop. Put on your happy face and make some ching.

When designing your booth take a good close look at how you are going to set up, load, and unload. These movements can tire you out before you even get to show time. Consider if you are going to be out on your own or do you have help?

What type of transportation will you have? All vehicles have their drawbacks; maneuvering for setups or breakdowns. Everyone has the same goal at the same time, get in or get out. Don't think you are limited by not having a truck or van. Just design your setup around the mode of transportation available.

Try to load most of your displays at home. Keeping in mind that you have to lift and jockey them.
Everything else is packed in clear plastic bins. These bins can last forever and you can see into them.

Your display design is always being built. While you are out, keep looking for new material to work with. Have an eye open for garage sales, trash nights.

America has a wealth of resources at our fingertips.

One of the most inexpensive and best display mediums is crib racks. They usually can be found for free. Add a couple of hinges or bungees and you're in business. You now have an excellent lightweight strong hardwood display with almost nothing invested! Lattice panels, in 4x8 sections are also another excellent material to work with. Again, think commando style, light, well equipped, and fast!

Here is another great idea, driftwood. Spend a day, along a shore picking some of natures best display material finished by the elements. If there is no water where you live, try looking for some decent tree roots. Clean them up, whamo; you have got a decent conversation piece. Shutters and ladders work out well. There are also some very good professional companies that will design and build displays to your specs. The Internet is an excellent source locator for connections. If you're not online most libraries should be or have resource libraries in hard copy. The more quality time you spend on your booth design and layout. The more familiar you will be in your element when it's ShowTime!

Let's talk about how tents framework and how they go together. Sooner or later you are going to do a show outside. Are you going to invest in a vender's tent, or use a summer shade tent? Some venders have built their framework to support a tarp. This type of set up is rigid when made properly. This framework can be part of their display inside and out.

When you use a tent, realize some inside shows will not let you use tent framework even if you have padded feet. Some folks that help produce shows only follow the rules that the building landlord requires. It is not worth trying to change the rules the morning of the show. Although tents inside are impressive, they can damage a beautiful floor, know the rules before the setup. While we are on the subject of tents let us talk about marking them with some type of identification, the framework, and all major parts. Depending on where you are, look at all the similar vender tents. How easy would it be to get your new tent mixed up with someone's slightly damaged tent?

As they say in the rodeo business. "Don't put yourself in the position to get your saddle swapped."

Tent designs vary from manufacture to manufacture. Just because you paid good money for the tent it doesn't guarantee that the tent will not leak. Buying a venders tent is not like a camping tent. There are many different types. Some types of tents leak by design. They are made just to keep out the sun and some of the elements. Look at the placement of the seams. Does the top cover just the top or is it a valence top? How do the sides connect to the framework? Do they go under the valence? Are the corners open? Be careful, some products can handle being a wet, others can't. When you are shopping for your tent ask other vendors questions about their tents. Some vendors don't like their tents. Others wish they had purchased more options or a different color canopy. White is the safest. It doesn't change the look of your product. If you pick a purple canopy your product may take on a purple hue. Heavy canvas does not let in any light. You are going to be in the dark, this may be very good if you're selling lamps. Decorating the outside with flags or streamers is a good attention grabber. The more you can do to cause someone to look your way the better the chance they may stroll by for a closer look.

Next let's talk about securing the tent to the ground. Try to shy away from pounding large spikes into the ground. You never know if there are water lines or electricity below you. Regular small stakes may serve you well. Sand bags or cinder blocks are heavy. In most cases your display should be rigid enough to stay down without any staking. Try to trust the weather predictions. If there are no high gusty winds in the forecast let your displays hold the tent down. When you get to the show location see what the conditions are. Then make the necessary adjustments.

The framework used for most shows is made out of IMC 1-inch pipe. Good solidly held together with welded couplings and thumb set screws. This is called the rigid display. This setup takes somewhere around 20 minutes to complete. It is a good idea to also own the lighter type vender's tent that has an accordion framework. You can pull it out of a nylon bag. Have it set it up, in about 5 minutes you are building the display. Let weather conditions govern which tent you use. The rigid setup seems to be more stable with Mother Nature. Your set up time is crucial so it is your choice; try not to let laziness make your decisions.

We have talked about tents, tops, inside, outside, and weather.

Let's take look at what is going to go into this portable home of prosperity; the display. The display can make or break the product you are pitching. Very few treasures look good, shown on any old thing you found lying around.

Let's clarify this; any old thing can be an excellent showcase. Try to put some thought into what you are using. The product has to fit while looking good.

Think about this. You are selling your treasures off of a flimsy rack you purchased from one of the chain stores. When sales are slow, do you really need to wonder why? Now picture this, you have this rack that you painted and attacked with a glue gun. Now add some nice trims from the fabric store hardware store, or junk yard. The rack is now jazzed up a little. Some of your energy has also been bonded to the display. If you have hangers of some type cover them with a complimentary trim. Does this picture give more of an appeal to you? How about the treasure hunter? You don't want your display to look like you just threw off last winter's clothes, and then hung a retail product from them. Take a walk into a good chain store. Then compare what you have seen to a cheesy looking dollar store. Notice the difference in the displays. Your high quality stores that do well in sales have their displays balanced. The products look happy while giving you the impression that it lives there. Don't crowd the displays; keep them full but not crammed.

Try to have a hanging display that is alive and happy. The treasure hunter will be pleased and impressed with the delight before them.

There are many types of displays. Flat ones, vertical, 3D, horizontal, cascading, stand alone, you name it, there is a way to present it. Remember however you choose to offer your wares, experiment, practice, then listen for comments. Your customers are the best source for information. Their comments can be very helpful when trying to display or sell. A lot of people will say, even if it is under their breath what they liked about your booth or product. A lot of your products and displays will evolve from shoppers' questions and comments. There is a saying out in the field.

"There is nothing smarter than a customer".

Believe it… if they're not buying from you there is a problem. Watch them maneuver, look to see if they're squinting or stretching, is their nose wrinkled up? All of these body movements can tell you things.

Try to set up your displays up at home. Live in your display for as long as possible. Get to know your display it is your friend. Write down what you like or don't like about your friend. If you can't set up at home look for some real inexpensive show in your neighborhood. Pay the booth rent. Set up to take pictures. Go to this show to practice. You may even sell something. School gyms, churches are always a good place to practice. They have good hard floors with plenty of light. Gyms normally have lots of room to get some decent angles for pictures. Try to bring a ladder to stand on. Shoot some shots from above. This perspective gives an enlightened dimension. During all of this planning, pay attention to your feelings for doing the designing and layout. This part of the job, you really should enjoy. How you look to the public in retail, is as important as a chef presents the dishes at a fine restaurant. If it doesn't look good it won't taste good and it probably will not sell.

When you do two-day shows try to put some pictures out on the web. It is real in expensive today if you look around. Some providers give you one page and a web address for a few dollars a year. Not every server charges high dollars.
There is a lot of low cost, no cost posting venues out there. My site costs me $45.00 a year, plus $8.00 domain registration. If you do put up a web site, a lot of customers will go home and surf to your site. Putting out pictures of your recent show will get good

feedback. Customers like to see up to date photos.

Let's Not Be a Hungry Vendor

While thinking about going into business for yourself, you have to face some reality. There is a lot to owning and operating a business. Standing or sitting around collecting money is not the way it happens for most of us. It takes a lot of work. You need to understand that there is an amount of planning that should happen before you collect the money. From the time you come up with the idea, until the first dollar you collect, it is an undertaking. You have to have a product that will sell. Your product needs to be appealing to the shopper. A well balanced product with color, display, and pricing, are all key factors to success. Putting a lot of thought into the stages of product development is a very serious part for the overall completion of your dream.   When you lack in ambition, you're going to lack in sales. This is not an hourly job; you don't get paid when you're unproductive. You will get out of this business what you put into it.

"Come on in; let's look at sales techniques."

Over a period of time all of us will develop different skills for closing. Prequalifying is the first step in getting that sale. What I mean by prequalify is not what a car dealer or a real-estate agent would do. Here in the show business there is a big difference. What you want to avoid is deciding which shopper is going to buy from you just by looking at them. Getting good consistent sales requires more than just looking at someone. If you are the type of person that looks at the world in a negative way you must learn to stop thinking like that. If you have other thoughts in your mind besides positive ones, start practicing. Think and look only at the good side of things. To do well, you must only have politically correct thoughts while it is ShowTime. In your mind you are running for mayor of the show circuit. Tactfulness is where it is. From the time you make eye contact until the cash box goes Cha-ching, ching. It is up to you and your developing skills to get that sale. Getting eye contact is not always possible with a shopper. A lot of folks will not allow themselves that part of humanity. That is ok for them; remember it is you that should be ready to give eye contact. Shoppers don't have to. They have the money. No eye contact may be understood as, "Leave me alone, I'll let you know when I need something".

Give folks a chance to come into your space. After a few moments let them know something about the products they are looking at. A good opening line is, "Feel free to handle that". Or "What do you think about the color, isn't it wonderful?" Tell them what the item is made of, or used for. Try to exchange a few words. See if you can at least get an acknowledgment from them. Experience will help you with the next moves to a sale. If you can get a shopper relaxed enough to at least say a few words you could be on your way to a sale. Pay attention here, if you talk too much or give too much information your sale may go down the road. Never over do it, you want to keep sales moving. If people are hanging around in your booth new sales may be missed. Deciding when a shopper needs to be left alone or made to feel welcome is something that takes practice, so practice, practice, and practice. Having a few good opening lines is a must. There are shoppers, there are browsers, making them customers is up to you. The only way to get more out of a show is, knowing how to work the crowd. At one show, your displays will sell the crowd. Ten seconds later you must sell yourself as well as the product.

There are the shows where you won't be able to sell at all, figure out why. Crowds can take on a mindset, shoppers are there but no buying is going on. The show circuit has seasoned travelers as well as people that don't get out much.

Let's not be a hungry vendor. If you're pushy you'll push the shoppers right into the next booth. Being overly helpful can be understood as,

"I don't want to make money; I just want to hear myself talk". Don't let them know you're hungry. You need to be in the frame of mind that allows you to handle the shoppers with a feeling of confidence. The reason you are there is to help the shoppers find that special gift.

Shoppers can be made to feel that they are missing something if they don't buy from you. The more you sell the easier it will become to have this confidence. Attitude is important, the right attitude you have to develop. Being a professional is work. You don't have to push yourself until it hurts, just enough to keep trying. You need drive to survive. Acting like a hungry vendor in the retail market is dangerous, especially if you are in a specialty area. In some sales markets being hungry is essential to surviving.

If you were selling medical equipment, industrial sales, or advertising being hungry may help. Trying to get to the head of the line in a rat race is important.

Here, it is different. Sure we want the sale. Yes, we want to be helpful. In our business there is no sales manager that wants all of the money that there is in the whole world in one day. Take your time and enjoy your shoppers.

Be ready. Be there. Be invisible. Retail specialty items can be tricky. You are not a major retail chain.

The chains have their program down to collecting money at the register. That did not happen overnight. A lot of planning thought, and caring went into their business. They now have it down to a person that knows very little about what is going on collecting money. Our goal as vendors is to be at least one step above them. We own our business. We know what is going on, as well as being able to make a decision without having to call someone. This is called good service. We have an American made product. How many products do you see on the markets like yours? It is up to you to swing the dollars to the economy's pocket. We are the backbone of this great nation. We are not afraid to work. We don't pay our workers fifty cents a day then send them home to no running water. Our business represents our heritage. When shoppers buy from us, they are buying a piece of America!

Closing at a show is exciting. Once you figure out how to work the crowd, and when to work your booth. You'll start to getting steady sales. Bringing busy work will relax you. Having some movement will attract glances. Try chatting up the vendors near you. Once you have activity, crowds tend to drift towards it.

Most shoppers are at shows because they like them. Our shoppers go to retail stores because they have to. They come to us because they want to. We have an advantage over the chains, use it. The best thing you can do for yourself is to be a confident vendor. Buyers don't buy from losers. Upbeat and happy will attract the best shoppers. If your booth is spiffy, you're spiffy.

"Come on in folks, I've got what you are looking for. Buy a piece of me when you buy one of my shopper's delights." People will sometimes buy product from you just because you made them feel something while they were browsing.

The show circuit is robust with good people, buyers, sellers, talkers, introverts, extroverts, the list is endless. Plug in, hang on, we're off to the next jump.

It's about enjoyment

While picking your show destinations, you need to put some thought into your route. How far are you willing to go, in distance and commitment? There are a lot of factors to consider. Are you going to start locally or jump in feet first and travel America? When selling in various states there may be different laws for vendors. It is your responsibility to know the law. Being smart and knowing the area you are in is what makes you a professional. Be legal for the location you are in. There are some interesting stories about vendors being caught selling without proper licenses or tax certificates. If you are supposed to collect some sort of tax, do it. It doesn't matter if you agree with tax laws or not. When you are selling, collecting money, bartering, whatever you want to call it. You are engaging in commerce. You are using public roads, spending paper money; therefore you are using the system. If the system requires you to collect a tax, do it. When you have customers that complain about the tax, tell them that,

"You don't charge a sales tax you collect it. If you have a problem with that, write to your legislatures about it."

We as an America can change our government with a hand full of votes. The G.W. Bush election proved that.

It's about enjoyment. It's about fun. Being an American engaged in commerce is a privilege. Agree or not with me it is your right. Get tax problems, you have got serious problems. Count on your fingers how many countries in the world you could live in that you could go out into the environment to find raw materials. Then manufacture and sell without having any serious problems. Be glad all the government wants is a tax. Keeping good records is essential to making more than a few dollars at a time.

Think of what you are selling, a few bucks of your product, bringing a steady cash flow. No matter how slight it is, you're making money. While doing something most people could never do, designing a product, marketing it, and then selling it.

"Wow, we are an industry. You are now a member of the backbone of a capitalist economy."

Welcome to small business America, the number one employer. No halfwit boss telling you what to do next. I'm sure you know the type.

You may be in another situation and just never seem to get a break and land a good job. You are now finally getting smart, make your next job. Give folks a good product and decent knowledgeable service, you're there.

"Hey, you want a new truck, van car, no credit no problem."

There are ways to get started in America. Go out and get a Penny's card or gas card, you name it, give it a try. Establish a credit history, use the system, it is there for you. This is America; pick out your vehicle to take you to your future. Make the commitment to better yourself. If you allow yourself not to be mobile, you're limited. Limited means you are going to have to design your product and layout, to work with some type of public transportation. Is that a problem? It depends on how resourceful you are. How bad do you want this income? We are talking about history here. A lot of Americans regardless of limitations have done it. The list is endless; add your name to it.

Do you want flexibility? Would you want to blame everyone around you for your situation? Capitalism works very well in this country.

The product you are going to sell should fit into your lifestyle. Being a show vender, selling, promoting your goods and services becomes a driving force in your life. When you work at a craft, time will become exciting. Having enough of it organized will be your challenge. A good indicator is your stomach. If it feels good do it.

Look around you for raw materials. Remember pet rocks? There was a real simple product to produce. The pet rocks took the market by storm, short lived but they did sell, lots of them too!

I hear tell they are bringing big bucks on EBay.

How about making up peat moss planting kits? Sell germinating plants. All you have to know is what is growing in the pots. That information is written on the seed packet. Logically, the more diversified the product line, the better chance for sales. Herbs are always a hit. They can be grown in a relatively small space. When certain types mature they don't need a lot of room.

The number one hit seems to be wood. If it collects dust someone will have to have it, for that special spot. Dried flower arrangers may argue with this point. The objective is to keep the product at the disposable income level. If it causes an impulse it will cause a sale. An extra $10.00; $ 20.00; $30.00 is where it is at. When you approach the $ 30.00 mark, it has to be quite spiffy.

This is a feat to be proud of. Yes, there are lots of folks with more than $ 30.00 in their pocket. If you are trying to sell to the niche market the percentage of happy shoppers leaving your booth may be lower. Think I am wrong … Take a trip through a major retailer. Check pricing, the larger portions of inventory are below $ 30.00.

That is why I am always stressing, "It's about enjoyment". You have to design a product, package it nicely to sell it. Most of us have to produce these items somewhere in our home. It may become an infringement or a welcome addition to your lifestyle. Shoppers delights will be drying on your kitchen table, bedroom, bathroom, you pick the real estate. Something will be there. Part of your product design should incorporate neatness and organization. When you design and manufacture in drudgery it will show up in the overall feel of your booth. Be happy while you work. Do whatever it will take to keep happy thoughts. Try to clean as you go. Break down production into simple logical steps. Try to do like cuts together. Make jigs to hold things the same way every time. Wear dust/vapor masks when needed along with surgical type gloves. Think of what solvents do to surfaces. Imagine what they could be doing to your organs. Chronic or acute exposure to chemicals/dust can develop into a serious problem. Take the time to use safety glasses, gloves, coveralls, proper venting, whatever it takes. Cut down your exposure times and levels any way you can. Doing something is better than nothing.

If you have tedious tasks, try to do as many as you can at one time. Set aside blocks of time for these responsibilities. The more of these types of things you do together the faster and more proficient you will become. There is no right way; it is what works for you. Try different ways to do a step, you may discover a time saving move. Maybe there is a way to make one task less aggravating.

Try to make a labor saving device or buy a good tool, this should be #1 on any list. Always try to obtain the highest quality equipment. When you buy cheap tools they can be very frustrating when they don't work well or not at all.

Always try to take some money that you have made and invest it in repairs or something new to your inventory. Well functioning tools operating safely are invaluable to the longevity of your business. In most cases try to use tools that have more than one use. Like a multiple tipped screwdriver, adjustable wrenches, high quality socket set. A nice lightweight battery powered drill is a sure bet.

If you be just getting started, or you have been doing it a while, try to make good high quality products. Making sure they are packaged and marked properly. This is basic retail here. The majority of Americans like to see prices on the items they are looking at. You can go to some shows and see vendors haggle with customers for goods that are not marked. For the most part Americans are uncomfortable wondering what the price is. Our lifestyles have been made very simple. Giving us too much to think about may cause us to bolt for the sunlight. A lot of folks are always looking for a reason to buy themselves something. At the same time they feel guilty for doing it. To have to ask for a price or how to care for it may be too much for the shopper to think about. When you have simple cards made up for each item, shoppers will feel at ease. They may be more inclined to ask you a few questions. Once this happens your chance for the sale will increase.

"Make sure the treasure is marked, and displayed properly."

You are only going to get a percentage of the sales available at each show. You will never get all the treasures hunters, only a percent.

That's why "It's about enjoyment." Do not push too hard or get into someone's face. Working your booth instead of sitting is important. Stay busy, stay happy, and leave all your baggage at home. Do not tell anyone coming into your booth your problems or complaints. Happy thoughts only, anecdotes, stories, you come up with pleasant thoughts.

Some folks for whatever reason like to be left alone. Pay attention to body language, smile and study the customer. If they seem fidgety go look for something to do. Remember some people need the 10x10 space to themselves. Always give them what they need. Be it space or conversation study your booth and learn it.

A nice little trick I learned while selling timeshares was to carry a small recorder in my pocket. Record yourself trying to sell your product. Play the conversations back, decide if your pitch is something that works and makes sense. Listen carefully to see if what you are saying has anything to do with selling the product. Remember Americans like things simple. Do not give them too much to think about. Let a friend or acquaintance listen to the tape. See what other people have to say about how you are handling yourself while trying to sell. Shoppers are the best indicators of your success. If you're not selling, something is wrong. Don't get upset if you go out and have a few bad days, they are normal, especially if you're just getting started. Selling is a craft in itself and takes careful planning. While you are sharing your sales pitch, taping it, discussing it remember; outside influence is not always the best influence. People who have never tried to strike out on their own may not be the best advice givers. It never hurts to go out and talk about what you are doing, that's more practice for you. Try to remember your interest, knowledge; determination will bring home the bacon.

Write up your sales pitch for your products. Always adjust your pitch for the situation, while saying the same things all the time. After a while it will become second knowledge. This way you will never have a problem remembering what you told someone. You should keep on adjusting your pitch until your sales are steady at the level you want. If you have a good product that is priced to sell, it will. If sales are low there could be something wrong and it may be you. To do well in any business, everything must be free flowing. Practice, practice, practice, the only way to do well is become professional. All movements, thoughts have a purpose while, "It's Show Time".

For some people it comes easy, others it takes the desire to learn, to train, it takes work. If you put the time into it you will make it. Don't ever quit. Our lives are full of crossroads just keep crossing them. Ever hear of the product

WD-41? Well I am told that it took 40 tries to make it right. Suppose it took eighty tries. So what, we would just be using WD-80. No one would be the wiser, right?

Your Business Development

Once you decided to join the show business, strategy comes into play. Having a plan that works for you and is right for your situation is important. As you work with your plan it should change with time as well as experience. Your business plan should point you in a direction that is all. You should never do a show where there was not some form of improvement noticed. Sometimes you will meet very special people, or figure out another way to display your goods. When you are at a show use the time to learn your craft, the craft of selling.

The business portion of the show business is where most of the problems crafters have. They make good products. Have a wonderful tent with a well-designed display. They don't really understand the marketing side. There is the customer-product development system. In this area you are laying the corner stone to go on. You have to build a solid base of business principles. A major problem a lot of us have is; how to transfer the relationship of ideas to money? Think about how you want to be remembered after a stranger spends some special moments with you. Are all your motives monetary based? Money, related to comfort is printed on paper, Yankee Green Backs. This paper can buy you a lot. It can also misdirect you.

What you are making, selling, collecting money on has a relationship to paper. You are making a tangible product from raw materials. This forms a basis for the paper money economy.

There is no dollar economy without a raw material conversion to finish goods sale. This is where you fit into the system. In colonial times producers of finished goods always found a way to establish themselves in the colonies. Countries cannot live on imports alone. Goods need to be manufactured locally, and then sold. You cannot have a solid paper economy if you only import.

A fair deal for you and the shopper will aid you to a successful craft business. Don't try to make all the money there is in one day. If your product is not selling face reality, something is wrong. Ask yourself is the price too high, too low? How is the market I'm in? Is it right for me? Does my breath stink? Look in the mirror and smile. Is what you see what you think you look like? What you should try to understand here is; if you only have one tooth make sure it is polished. Try to figure out what is going on with your product. There are reasons why you're making sales or not. Apply this principle all the time. Look at how you handle your business; it will shape your future. The more successful entrepreneur always makes people associated with them money, with little or no problems. Shoppers should receive a high quality product at a fair price. Always set your pricing so you can sell it. Be able to retail or sell to a distributor for a percentage off retail. If you can't afford to sell the product with an amount going to an outside party it may be the wrong product for you or your market. Remember you have hidden partners such as the IRS, operating expenses, and raw materials. The list will become quite impressive for business partners you didn't know you had.

Making money is all percentages. Uncle Sam gets some. The utilities get a little. You have to buy or obtain raw materials. There are standard operating costs to running your show business. Like it or not they are there. You have to load them in and add your share to the overall price. If you can't be fair to yourself, your shoppers, or wholesalers, you are going to be a flash in the pan.

Once you are out on the show circuit being a resource is helpful. Let some secrets out to shoppers or venders that will help them. If your product is good enough people will start trying to copy it. Remember you are a professional;

you will always be ahead of your competition. There are stories of venders not letting shoppers know where they are buying some raw materials. Another good one is about a store not telling a shopper who supplies the craft item for fear of losing a sales commission. If a store refers a shopper to you for a custom order or a modification, have a prior commission agreement. Being knowledgeable with useful information is advantageous for your reputation. It is a good thing for people that come in contact with you to have a pleasurable experience. Being at odds with peers or shoppers is not where you want to be.

The most important portion of your business is how you treat everyone. Pay your various fees. Go out and find an honest tax advisor. One that knows and understands the tax laws as well as bookkeeping. If you think you are going to make money by cheating your suppliers, taxman, shoppers, you need to wake up fast. Do the best you can at playing by the rules. If you're using the banking system, keep decent records. The last thing anyone needs is tax problems pointing to cheating. An honest tax advisor will not allow a client to cheat. Our tax laws are complicated as well as changing. You're better off having a professional working with you. Take a look at this country. An awful lot of businesses make out very well operating within the system. Keeping decent records for tax purposes helps you as well. There are a lot of small businesses that would not be doing so well if keeping records was an option. How are you going to know how much to charge if you don't know what it cost to produce? You have transportation costs, meals, raw materials, and office expenses. The list can be endless or short. It is up to you. Operating costs will really eat into gross sales.

When you track operating costs eventually you will get a feeling for the prices you charge. If you have a product that sells for $35.00, it costs $25.00 to get to the public, is that $10.00 net worth it? Let's break down the costs. We use the 10% rule here. A product that retails for $35.00 should have less than $3.50 in raw materials. These are real numbers used for illustration purpose; your actual costs can vary.

```
$35.00   item
-3.50   raw material
$31.50
- 3.00   box
$28.50
-  .15   tag
$28.35
-  .20   bag
$28.15
- 5.00   machine time
$23.15
-13.00   ½ hr labor
$10.15   gross profit
```

All of these costs have hidden costs. Remember your hidden partners? Well, here are more. So now you are down to approximately $10.15 gross profit left from the original $35.00. With that $10.15 left you have to pay income taxes, booth fees, office expenses, road charges, heat, lights, meals, etc. Where did all the money go? See how easy it will be to make or lose money. Folks this is no joke here. Know what it costs to get to the show as well as understand it. Don't waste precious production time making things you can't load standard operating costs into. Unless you just need some quick cash, then by all means, crank'em out baby. You see, you are in charge; you own your own company. It is your business you can do what you want.

Freedom

At times during all civilizations there has been moments that are ripe for harvest. The Internet has evolved into a worldwide communication device. Major corporations are "Simplifying their work force". The elder Baby Boomers are being purged from the corporate pipeline. We have an opportunity that has presented itself like never before in modern society. We can make a prosperous living by using the basic skills we have gained while working, playing, and balancing our checkbooks. There are millions of Boomers out there that are going to be retired soon. They are on the front end of an investment cycle. Do your homework; find out what they may need. Most of us will live way beyond our ability to live off of the investments we made. Having some extra cash flow may circumvent that. I personally know a few people that went back to work out of sheer boredom.

There are a lot of folks out there that have worked hard for their after tax dollars. They are the ones that are the hardest to sell to. They have money for what they need or want. The mainstream media, as well as retail sales have ignored this market. Trendy things that are mass-produced in third world economies are unpredictable with our market. The me generation won't touch these folks, except to sell them some type of miracle drug that may cause side effects. The product we sell has no side effects. Our folks can be made happy by showing them a decent product for a fair price. We are good people that work hard to supply a fair high quality product.

To be a vender is to be a gypsy. All through history travelers have had something the masses wanted. From the days of traveling brush salesman to cosmetics, good products, good services, brings good sales.

Our nation has based its existence on "Freedom". Freedom of choice, freedom of speech, Freedom to travel and sell! Don't think you have freedom? Go to Boston, go to a park and give a speech. They can't stop you. America is free, maybe not perfect, but free. We don't have to grovel for a paycheck. Here in America dreams can be built. All of us get to die, let's take one more step and live! This is the new simplified world. Take all you have learned, pick up all the dimes that the me generation has stepped over to make dollars.

Starting your own business will change the way you look at life. At times it may feel like you are pushing a big rock up a hill. Keep pushing; you'll get to the top. When you are tired, rest. If you get frustrated find something that will divert some attention for a while.

This book has been written as a guide to aid all of us in planning out our lives. Not all the answers are found here. Some things have been overlooked as well as left out. It is up to you to find out what works for you, as well as what will not work. The intent in sharing this information is to help you save some time and mistakes with a few things that I've learned over the years.

Feel free to share some of your experiences as well as ideas to others. Over time some of your customers will become good friends. When you start to make friends from customers and vendors you will be on the right track. Feedback will be important for you to update your skills

"Good luck, may God bless you.

About the Author

In 1980 we drove through Lake Placid, N.Y. to visit the Olympic sites. It was an enjoyable visit as well as breath taking.

My wife and I always wanted to live year round in the Adirondack Mountains. Upstate New York has a lot to offer independent small business. One obstacle is the winters. They are cold and long. Some industries need winters. Lake Placid seemed ideal for a 3-season business. A year later we received a letter in the mail to visit a time-share at the Lake Placid Club. While up there visiting, there was a snowstorm and we got snowed in for the night. After dinner, while wandering around, we found a beautiful little shop that needed some TLC. The next thing we knew we were with an architect designing our craft store. By the summer of 1982 we were open full speed ahead. For the main product line we decided to manufacture weavings. Our shop had cones of yarn as well as working looms. The shop sold retail, and took custom orders. During the summer months we traveled locally and did a few craft shows. After five years of trying to make it in Lake Placid we had to leave. Most of our customers were from the Albany /Saratoga area, we decided to settle there. We now occupy a property that use to be a small engine repair shop with a house. At any one time we normally have 15 working looms as well as mountains of colorful yarn to wet the palette of any craft/artisan. The craft show income is supplemented by a few commercial accounts that send checks regularly.

From June until December we travel the upstate craft show circuit selling our wares. This mobility enables us to enjoy the beauty of upstate New York while making some good friends. We are now in our 29th year and have plans for another 20 years. At times it has been hard. But when you get a smile or a sale from a special customer all the problems melt away.

Finding something we both liked to do together have made us a happy family. Yes, we traveled with 2 children. We had to help each other as well as work. It can be done. Our kids are up early, ready to go. We always try to pick shows where kids can have some fun. One of us is always running the booth; the other is sightseeing, or swimming. Imagine a summer where part of your job is to lay around at a beach and drink spring water, while spending some time with your kids! Sounds kind of tough ah?

"See you at the next jump"

Glossary

Bungees – rubbery flexible cords with hooks or balls on the end

Cha-Ching - what goes into your pocket or bank account.

Closing - what you need to do, to get the Cha-Ching

Gross profit- what you think you have left.

Jump - a carnival term used to reference the next show location

Labor rate - What is charged or added on to the cost of doing business.

Machine time - what it costs to operate, maintain, store, and replace if necessary. Can usually be calculated by the projected 5-year cost of buying and or servicing the equipment divided by the number of hours used.

Me generation - not necessarily tied to a specific age group. A product of modern society as well as technology. A group of people that do not care about the whole village, only the part that they live in. They rarely volunteer for anything.

Net profit - dollars that are left after you pay all the known and unknown partners. What you can fold up that is yours and fits into your wallet. Something that makes you smile.

Pitch- A developed train of thought to bring someone or a group to a conclusion.

Prequalify – A skill that will be learned over time. A walk you take your shopper on.

Show Schedule – An organizational tool that is very important to you and your customer. It will enable you to find yourself in the future. It will help the customer find your goods.
Include a list of dates and locations where you will be vending.
    Example; postcards, handouts with email, phone number, web site information.

Vendor Survival Kit

WATER

Meds

Use tobacco products away from the booth

Multi tipped screwdriver

Adjustable wrench

Push pins / tacks

Note cards, gift cards, etc for signs, notes etc.

Pliers

Flashlight

First aid kit

A Cooler with healthy food. Shows usually don't require food vendors to be as high quality as the craft vendors.

Wipe-ez

Sunscreen

Maps of the area

Camera/phone

Bungees

Tax ID or number

Colored markers/pens

Hammer

Good attitude

Battery powered drill

Tent

*

*

*

*

With love and devotion, thank you Lori for being my friend, my wife, my business partner.

Front cover and chapter photographs courtesy of Lori

Finishing touches by Uncle Mike McManus, Thanks..!

Thank-you Shorty and Seal at Createspace
Thank- you Amazon for making your company
and services
available to us self- publishers

Notes

Notes